AF603976

My Eyes Are Barely Open

some seasonal reflections

by Andrew Wesselhoff

This one's for you, dear reader.

Who I am is who you are.

“Never trust a musician
Who plays with their eyes open
All the good shit happens when they’re closed”

- John Craigie, *‘I Wrote Mr. Tambourine Man’*

A Note About the Cover

I have slowly come to accept that my eyes will never be fully open.

You see, my right eye is actually legally blind, and is always bearing a somewhat permanent squint. And I never wore glasses until middle school, so the left one would always end up doing all the work. I have a theory that over time my right eye grew accustomed to its uselessness, and my eyelids learned to hide it. And because my left eye was overcompensating, it began to hide itself as well. To make matters worse, I could never wear contacts because I just physically couldn't open my eyes wide enough to drop them in. And anytime I smiled, my eyelids would frustratingly close even further. So because of this, I've always been drawn to large, round glasses to mask my tiny eyes.

I used to be quite self conscious about all of this. I actually used to hate both of the photos of myself on the front and back covers of this book.

They perfectly captured everything I hated about my eyes and my smile. But, the fact remains that they're also photos of an insecure 17 year old sharing his genuine smile, despite his insecurities.

It's been about eight years or so since these old pictures were taken. Eight years is a long time.

I'm 25 now. I started writing these poems about four years ago, and you're holding the third volume in this series of little poetry books.

Four years is also a long time. So much can change (and does change) in just one single day. And four years is almost 1500 days.

After these seasonal reflections and countless rhymes, I have learned to love and accept that 17 year old, insecurities and all. In fact, he is here with me now, proudly bearing that same goofy smile, while this 25 year old types this sentence.

My desire for the poems and the story they tell within these pages is that they might help you to do the same. I hope you can discover how the same truth that once brought despair can grow into a resolute cry of self-acceptance, only through a slight change in tone.

My eyes are barely open.

Table of Contents

Still Yearning 81

Still Healing 121

Table of Contents

Still Drowning

book six

I'd Rather Be Hopeful

I really hope we're growing
ever closer
to that which we can never know.

I really hope our eyes are opening
ever wider
until the fateful day they close.

But maybe it's all just a story
I tell myself,
to feel better about myself.

Maybe
it's always been in our nature
to believe in false hope.

Either way,
I don't know if I'll ever know
the Truth.

But I'd rather be hopeful than miserable.
Wouldn't you?

Embellishment

Every story
is a bit embellished.

Reality
is never *that* poetic.

Tire Pressure

I hit a pothole on the way to work
this morning,
the kind that's just impossible
to avoid.

My whole car shook.
But by some
tiny miracle,
my tire stayed inflated.

My whole life had led
up to that moment.
My whole being depends
on tire pressure.

Back to Shore

For a while, the tide
brought me back to shore.
So I walked for miles
with a stranger I adore.

We talked for hours
in the sand,
discussing the sea,
the land, and everything between.

Can you feel the water
moving foundations?
We're cresting, falling,
crashing, and everything between.

Now the tide,
has come again
so I began to cry,
as one does.

And this strange man just wept with me.

Prescriptions

The right one is legally blind;
he lives with
a somewhat permanent squint.

So his brother must atone
for inherited sins.
Eventually, he grows bitter;
a somewhat natural progression.

So the other grows defensive
of his narrow perception
while simultaneously slandering his partner
for the very same sin.

And their argument will persist
until the mediator gives them a prescription;
a necessarily ignorant solution.

By sharing lenses,
our uniquely broken perceptions are blended.
By sharing lenses,
we are often avoiding cathartic confrontation,

By sharing lenses,
we are sharing pretense.

Frames

I'm always paranoid
that my glasses rest
crooked on my face.

But sometimes I forget
that they're even there at all.

What I see as flawed
you might see as sublime.
But we all have frames
in peripheral sight.

Crooked or not,
we see through our own lenses.

Metaphors

Heaven's just a metaphor
to help me close my eyes.

Heaven lets me wander,
Love will be alright.

Love, we'll be alright.

Something To Cry About

I’ve always got
something to cry about.

I’m always just
about to break down.

And it’s my suspicion
that you are too.

I just wish I knew how
to cry with you.

Purgatory Dr.

I took a walk to clear my head,
it didn’t work.

One neighbor’s grass
was green and watered

while his neighbor’s
was dry and barren.

So I couldn’t help but wonder,
“Is it the same inside?”

as I walked down purgatory drive…

A Sacred 'Yes'

Breathe deeply
dear friend.

There still might be
a sacred 'Yes'
in all things.

Whittled

Hold on, as tight as you can
until you can't anymore.

Then let it go.

All I've learned, whittled down to this:
It all means nothing without

a little hope,

a little longing, a little crying,
and a lot of dancing through it all.

Perhaps the divine masterpiece
is resiliency of the human soul.

The Fallacy of Identity

Which son was the prodigal one?
It had to be you, because
who I am is who I am not.

So I pushed against until the walls dissolved
until I was naught
but prodigal and wasted.

My dear brother, I am so sorry.
I don't want to keep fighting.
I don't want to resist anymore;
who I am is who you are.

I thought I knew what faith was,
I thought I knew who I was,
I thought I knew right from wrong.

But in all my resistance,
I've never found the difference
between the two of us.
Instead I keep finding
more reasons to love.

The Song of the Valley

The red rock is speckled, green.
The green is covered, white.

The river runs, right through me.
Clouds cover us; still we shine.

Can you hear the song of the valley, deep?
It's not words she sings, listen with your eyes.

Collective Melody

I am only but the song you sing with me.

The image of God is collective melody.

Look Closer

The mountain is moving;
if you look close enough
she is moving you.

The wind is singing;
if you listen hard enough
she is singing to you.

An Already Abundant Life

O Seeker,
there is nothing to seek.
  She already speaks.

Ask and you shall be given
one answer:
  seek and you shall find
  another seeker.

There is nothing to earn,
and nothing to find
  but a mirror,
  reflecting an already abundant life.

Transcendence by the Dumpsters

'Music is everything right now,'
he said as he sucked on a cigarette
that was slowly killing him.

He looked off into the distance as he said it,
as if he was looking for something
bigger than him
to agree with him.

'Yes it really is,' I replied with a smile,
after letting him search for a little bit.

And just for a moment,
we escaped the world around us
by the dumpsters.

Homes

The home we lost
was the home our parents built.

The home we build
is the home our children lose.

But the home we will find
is hidden in my grandpa's smile.

Pipe Dreams

I asked you,
'What are we holding on to?'
  but it was mostly rhetorical.

I'm still
drowning,
  still learning how to let go.

I've got
pipe dreams
  of something universal.

Prerequisites

Forgiveness is but
a prerequisite.

Redemption will come
when it's forgotten.

Kinesics

It's never the words
or the language.
It's the way you say it.

Are you smiling
or frowning?
Are your arms crossed?
Can you look me in the eyes or not?

It's never the rhythm
or the lyrics.
It's the way you sing it.

I don't give a damn
if you're out of tune or in the wrong key
if it moves you, it moves me.

Dominoes

I’ve been so careful,
but small worlds are dominoes.

Now it’s falling apart,
And I can’t help but laugh.

It’s a big world,
it’s a good life.

Small Screens

I was watching
a stupid tv show to pass the time
and it made me cry.
A lot chokes me up these days.

But sometimes I feel like I'm wasting time
watching these stupid tv shows.
We only have so many days, you know?

I often wonder where we'll go when we die.
I'll never know until I'm out of time,
I guess.

Until then,
I guess I'll just watch another episode
and waste some more time...

I don't know if I really want eternal life,
there's only so many tv shows to watch.

The Way I Believe in You

I want to believe in God
  in the same way I believe in you.

I don't need to prove your existence
any more than you need to prove mine;
  our eyes are glistening
  in the same light.

Where there is connection,
  there is movement;
where there is movement,
  there is conversation;
where there is conversation,
  there is God.

In My Glove Compartment

My most sacred possessions
are a bunch of old CDs
in my glove compartment.

I never play them
or even look at them, for that matter.
Most of them are probably
scratched and broken anyway.

But its such a comfort to know
that they're always there.

All I am
is the music I hold.

It's the Same Celebration

Pentecost is Shavuot.
It's the same celebration.

The names we give it
are not that important.

If you are breathing,
you know the spirit's movement.

So breathe deeply, dear friend.
Our eyes are barely open.

Seasonal Reflection

I tend to feel everything at once.
But with seasonal reflection,

my heart waits for my mind
to catch up.

I'm still learning
how to sing
what's already been sung.

Still Dancing

book seven

It Rained at the Celtic Festival, ...

and the redhead
danced in the rain
with the fiddle
and her bare feet.

She couldn't dance
her fears away,
and still she danced
anyway.

She was hiding,
she was glowing.

Interpolations

Maybe
Summer is interpolating
Winter's melodies.

Maybe
their motifs are
Fall and Spring.

Summer Days

Summer days
romanticized.

In good faith,
we are compromised.

Her freedom blurs and fades,
still sanctifies.

Mourning always wakes
with softer eyes.

Summer Nights

Summer nights,
still light, after 5.

Sharing laughter,
sharing songs,
sharing smiles.

My hand glides
outside; 45
miles per hour.

And the bass blows out my speakers
as the wind blows between my fingers.

I am learning how to fly.

Suspension of Disbelief

I am the willing fool,
with that stupid grin.

You know the one, where
my eyes are barely open.

My hair is growing curly again.
The air is getting heavy again.

And still we float away
all the same.

Our disbelief is suspended,
this summer will never end.

Like Learning to Sing

Like learning to sing,
Love closes her eyes
sometimes

and every rhyme
is revived
by its own futility.

A tranquil disguise.

Heartbeats

There is freedom
in knowing
you cannot fail
because you cannot get close.

So trade your words for 'woahs.'

There is freedom
in knowing
our hearts will never beat together
but they can still get close.

So dance steady, sway slow:
 between 60 and 100 BPM.

Past Lives

This road is lonely,
this road is long,

but every now and then,
there are a few sacred moments when
it doubles back in on itself,

overlaps, collapses, and binds;
revealing itself as hardly a road at all.

This happened tonight,
in the middle of our favorite song.
You can call it serendipity if you want.

But regardless, there she was.
A past life. Lost and found.
Familiar blue eyes in this massive crowd.

So we smiled, shared a tiny nod,
and then carried on singing.

Inaccurate Descriptions

To encounter a feeling
and fail to describe it
is all this amateur poetry is.

Experience
can only be shared with experience.

And yet,
inaccurate descriptions
are never meaningless.

Wedding Reception Reflections

Keep yourself in check
but don't forget
to forget
every now and then.

Let the movement
move
your soles.

Let the cards
fall
where they fall.

The only thing
that means anything
is dancing.

In Certain Light

In certain light,
black and blue will mix.

Still, neither color
is extinguished.

It might do us good
to remember this.

The General Dance

The only devotion
that Love denies
is where faith hides away;

  in exclusivity.

Like two partners
swaying in tender embrace,
together they fade

  in unity

but not uniformity.

The Catch

A cigar
and a beer
is all I need.

Everything else
is just a bonus prize.

But here's the catch:
I still need everything else
to realize it.

Let's do an experiment:
hold your breath
for just a moment.

Can you feel it?

A New New Testament

The words we cherished
are the words we will write
and the days we remember
are the days we become.

These pages have turned,
these pages have yellowed.
Maybe these pages will burn
with the rest of us
(if any burn at all).

It is finished,
it has always been finished,
but it is still being written.

A Desert Waltz

Your head rests on my chest.
Your heart beats with mine;
blessed desecration.

You're not like the rest.
As wise as a child.
As childish as a gentleman.

Ours is a rare friendship,
as sacred as it is common;
a well in the desert.

We are nothing more
than skin and bones,
songs and screams,
and incarnation.

Smoke Breaks

Meditating
  between hazy breaths.
She is missing
  from her cubicle desk.

Spiritual
  smoke breaks in the stairwell.
New psalms
  are burning in her lungs.

Idealism

You hope to find a wisdom
that you think your parents possess.

You hope to find a love and a passion
that only exists in movies.

You hope to find the future you imagined
as the present you're living

This hope is all well and good,
but it will amount to nothing
if you're still holding on to it
if and when you stumble upon
the wonderful disappointment
of the real thing.

Idiomatic

Most of this
is idiomatic.

So let yourself
defy definition.

Lose the letter,
find the spirit.

It's Just Breathing

All I have
I will lose again.

All I have lost
will soon be gained.

It's just breathing.

Fleeting Harmonies

You play your instrument
and I play mine.
For one fleeting moment
we harmonize.

And our need for answers
dissipates
during this momentary escape
(if it lasted forever,
nothing in us would change).

For this ephemeral eternity,
we participate
in this resonant current that binds and frees
all things.

Horatio's Eyes

In tragedy's wake,
he wrote a song of praise.
I never understood how that happened.
I don't think he did either.

True Bethel is hidden
in all of it or none of it.
I guess it all depends
on how you see it.

Sometimes,
I wish I could see through Horatio's eyes.

But alas,
all I will ever have
are mine.

Even God Looks Foolish While Dancing

Within this exhausting chase
of our own projections,
the rhythm of the race
still overwhelms.

There is no God
that is not
already dancing, like a fool
right where you're standing!

So what have you got to lose?

Play the fool.

Dinner on the Roof

We left our confrontations
disguised as conversations,
with mouths full of
stale and microwaved answers,

at the door with our shoes.

Instead we discussed how everything
is soaked and layered in grace,
with mouths full of
stale and microwaved dinner,

barefoot on the roof.

A Lonely King

Certainty is a lonely king,
living alone
in his castle of sand.

A single question
can unravel his fortress,
like a bucket full of water
poured playfully
onto your masterpiece
by your sister.

Don't get mad, kid.
She just wants to be included.
This is the way it's always been.

The left hand never knows
what the right is doing.

Why I Can Never Finish a Puzzle

I'm just no longer
that concerned
with answers.

When the puzzle is completed,
it is disassembled
and then goes back in the box.

The Importance of Catharsis

Give it life
Give it breath
Let it move
Let it through.

Bare your soul
to a trusted friend.
They will listen
if you look them in the eyes.

The words you actually exchange
will be irrelevant, if you've already
mustered the courage to speak your mind.

Real Language

Words are secondary
in most conversations.

Real language
is mostly communicated
through the eyes.

The Musician's Prayers

He doesn't pray much anymore,

or at least not how he used to.
Mostly, he doesn't see the need.

A good musician will listen
long before he even thinks about playing.

The Mundane

Oh, what grace
to see and to breathe
a new day
  with old eyes.

Oh, what grace
to give and receive
another second chance;
  another sunrise.

Oh, what grace
that I'm not always
in a constant state
  of epiphany.

Thank you Lord,
  for the mundane.

I Still Believe in Kaleidoscopes

Forever strangely intertwined.
Together, we suffer alone.

I'll live my whole life
as an extra in your show.

Maybe it's foolish,
but most of the time I still hope
that there is neither Gentile nor Jew,
and no separation.

Maybe it's naive,
but most of the time I still believe
in kaleidoscopes.

Supposedly Sacred

With all the data available,
and every possible experiment completed,
one man concludes that maybe all of it

can be sacred.

But with every passage analyzed,
and every verse memorized,
his brother still laments that it has all

been desecrated.

So what the hell makes a sacred thing?
What power separates heaven from hell,
and what do we make of these inevitable

spaces between?

I'm sure you've spent a lot of time in
supposedly sacred spaces,

on weekdays as well as Sundays.

What makes them different
from the desecrated ones?

Well, here's my conclusion
(and it's not much of one):

it doesn't matter much.

Maybe
every contradiction
is and always has been
dancing in tandem.

"But it does not matter much,
because no despair of ours
can alter the reality of things;
or stain the joy of the cosmic dance
which is always there.

Indeed, we are in the midst of it,
and it is in the midst of us,
for it beats in our very blood,
whether we want it to or not."

- Thomas Merton

The Designated Driver's Observations

The music frames
the doting couple
who pregamed way too hard.

He stumbles backward
while she leans forward.
When will they learn?

The space between
the sidewalk and his shoes
is infinite.
Every step is eternity.

She is aware. She is oblivious.
She is still dancing without him.
He will never know how much she blesses him.

Suspension of Belief

Nothing really matters.

Do you believe in God?
 It doesn't really matter.
  You're my sister.

Do you not believe in God?
 It doesn't really matter.
  I'm your brother.

Our belief is suspended.
 This summer is ended,
  until next year.

Still Yearning

book eight

Distortions

I've been chasing the dream
that something,
  anything,
can fulfill me.

But the longer I chase
the more discouraged I get.

So instead, I've been
prolonging the feeling of longing
  for fulfillment
for as long as I can.

But the longer it stays
the more distorted it gets.

Twilight

You're not sure when
you'll see her again
as the twilight lasts
a little bit longer.

So why the hell is it then
you can't hold her gaze
any longer?

You both look down
and away
feeling magnetized
to each other;

desperately trying
to delay this new chapter
a little bit longer,
bathing in the dying light.

Seasonal Blessings

Soon the river
will freeze over.

And then it will melt again.

There is no greater blessing.

Warm Regret

Every chapter and every number
is a valiant yet futile attempt
to make sense of chaos.

And yet, all that will remain in our last chapter
is the warm regret of knowing
we should have never been afraid of chaos.

The Individualist

The individualist
ironically loses himself quicker than most.
It's not worth it to go it alone.

Tragically ignorant
of the consequences
of his isolation,
he separates and defines
and separates and defines
and separates and defines
until it's too late,
and all that remains
is echoes, distortions
and a pair of lonely, sunken eyes.

Nonetheless,
when all is truly lost,
his fortress is still not safe
from the destructive grace
that will save us all.

Still Yearning

Headlights on the horizon
flickering off and on,
signaling some kind of
tiny flaming clues.

I'm still yearning
to see
these human constellations

not as a million
insignificant yet important
stories,

but instead
as simply one web of being.

Hidden Purple Heels

He dons his tie
but forgets his shoes.
A genuine lie,
an honest ruse.

Her purple heels
hide under white
while she drowns
in her lover's eyes.

This could symbolize
so many things,
but I think
she just likes purple.

There's really nothing that grandiose
about this moment,
or any other moment that will follow.
But I am still holding back tears.

Perhaps, the impossibly simple
is all we need to hold on to.

Placebos

We wanted it to mean something.
And so it did.

We told ourselves it was love
until it was.

Is that morally wrong?
Maybe.

But we're probably
in too deep
for that question to matter much anymore.

Playing with Fire

He's been here before,
but his eyes were wider
last time.

Still he risks another word,
knowing it will burn.

As he catches his breath
(hoping for sparks to catch),
he is dimly aware
this moment of anxious silence
is the kindling of friendship.

Three Minutes at a Time

For now we see dimly,
longing
for real sanctuary.

For now we sing
a dusty old hymn
with shiny new instruments,
and colorful new outfits.

For three minutes, we feel
through the facade.
Then it's gone.

This kingdom
is but a shadow
of what it could be.

A Desert Waltz II

Together we search the desert
for a well.
Together we brave the waves
of ourselves.

Crashing, colliding, breaking,
mending...
Changing, adapting, reaching,
grasping...

It's a fool's errand
to keep an old friend.

But something tells me
it's the only errand
that's worth anything
in the end.

What Makes a Good Story?

She whispered to me,

"if it was all glory,
would it still be a good story?"

as the light was fading.

Participations

It's not in our nature,
but it is always nurtured.

Nothing is given
before it is learned.
It's not 'original sin,'
it's participation.

So many men
are still yearning
for their father's pride.
For this reason,
pastors beget pastors
most of the time.

And maybe that's alright.

Autumn

In spite of all that fades away,
Autumn always hides a pretty face.

I just wish I could remember her name…

Our Great Comedy

All we are
is how we are remembered.

Our Great Comedy, however,
is that all is already forgiven
(and will therefore be forgotten).

Maybe our willingness
to laugh at this absurdity
is all that salvation is.

I'm No Soldier

I'm over war metaphors.
I'm no soldier anymore.

I fought,
I lost,
I found

that failure is the only teacher.
And she whispers
her riddle with a stupid grin:

'The ground is transparent.
The song is inherent.'

Just Passing Through

I am eternity
passing through.

Just like you.

Sober Mistakes

All the drunken lovers
are laughing in the wrong places
at the right times.

It's often quite easy
to mistake a joke
for a lie.

Especially when you're sober.

The Midnight Busker

The street is crowded and loud
and no one pays any attention
to the ones they walk with.

We are far from content
yet far from lonely,
like a good melody.

It's eleven thirty
and he's alone with 88 keys,
and our drunken company.

His tune is distorted
and overly long,
yet still true.

As I awkwardly
dropped a dollar
in his tip jar,

he didn't even look up.

The Medium Itself

Sometimes
the medium itself is the miracle.

Right now,
you are breathing in, and breathing out,
and that's incredible.

A Cosmic Stalemate

Everything changes
under the same stars.

We are on our way
to where we are.

The Existential Prayer

When these existential things persist
(as they do),
the mind descends, until all that's left
is a single repeated prayer,
spoken both by and to
no one in particular…

Are you holding on to
or hiding from
the idea of yourself?

Are you terrified
or comforted by
the sheer momentum
of this train of thought?

What if it's all just an ego trip,
and all we are is a tiny thing
trying desperately to prove its largeness?

Why can't we see this red thread
that supposedly connects us
to each other?

What makes me 'me'?
What makes you 'you'?

Where do I end
And you start?
Are we the current
or the river itself?
How can I face the truth
of my false self?

Lord, when you make us in your image,
are we literally reflected?

When you declare,
"I Am."
Do we reply,
"Am I?"

Between the Bookends

When we choose to simplify
and divide our existence
into highs and lows,
joy and suffering,
beginnings and endings,

what are we missing?

What happens
between the bookends?

Miracles, mostly.

Movements

Why must the camel bear his burdens alone
and assume we are all the same?

Why must the lion's rage run its course,
and leave so much despair in his wake?

In spite of all that fades away,
why does adolescence return anyway?

I could tell you why,
but you wouldn't be satisfied,
because it's not much of an answer.

But I can promise
all who seek
will surely find.

There is no arrival.
There is no destination.

There is only movement.

Dissolutions

When Ego meets Wisdom,
the child returns to play.

Listen close, and you'll hear him
laughing and lamenting
at the miraculous joke
that he doesn't exist.

Relearning and unlearning.
God is dissolving within.

Erosion

If I looked at yesterday
with tomorrow's eyes,
would I be ashamed
to testify?
Or would I be reclaimed
and sanctified?

No name can withstand
the march of time.
The rock of yesterday
is now the sand of the shoreline.

I know I can't meet your gaze tonight,
but I hope to meet you
by the water
someday soon.

The Ballad of Leaf and Stone

Every maple leaf on the weeping tree,
eventually falls to the red floor.
And the wind gently carries one lucky leaf
far, far away.

He is finally laid to rest by a park bench.
Here, he befriends a stone
who has only begun his journey.

The two unlikely friends converse
and ponder their purpose,
and as it begins to snow, they begin to fall in love.

But by the time the snow is gone,
Leaf has passed on.
Naturally,
Stone mourns his passing for quite some time.
Mourning is part of the journey.

And even though the pain of loss is always present,
Stone takes comfort in Leaf's final encouragements:

> *"Just like every leaf is carried*
> *far, far away,*
> *every stone erodes to the shore,*
> *and finds grace*
> *in her gentle waves."*

Ghosts and Gardens

I used to believe
wholeheartedly
in ghosts and gardens.

And in some ways I still do.

All the light we seek
is all the light we see.
Nothing is hidden
but our own face,
our own faith,

our own eyes.

To uncover the light in ourselves,
the light that unites us all,
we *must* learn to use this myth
as a mirror,

not as a wall.

A Mental Wound

It's a mental wound;
a personal truth,
a good intention,
a broken sentiment.

She believes
she's embodied
and free
only when she's immovable.

But it's always moving,
reflecting, refracting
and confusing.

It's a mental wound.
A mirror is never truthful.

A Litany of Rotations

Another great commission
Another silent frustration
Another vacant expression
Another false negation (and yet a true despair)
Another desecration
Another deconstruction
Another new translation
Another acclimation
Another realization
Another consecration
Another incarnation . . .

For a moment
there is freedom
that always was.
Until another wave comes.

Another separation
Another accusation
Another isolation
Another deprecation (and yet a true prayer)
Another divided nation
Another great commission
And another rotation…

With a deep sigh,
another wave passes by.
We need more time.
We need more time.

The Inadvertent Journey Inward

"Anywhere but inward!" I promised myself.

So I looked outward. I looked around.
I looked up. I partook.
And yet, I still found myself
mostly defined by arbitrary identity.

So soon enough,
I found myself
out of options, out of moves,
utterly exhausted and confused.

So I pondered. I deliberated.
I lamented for far too long
and not long enough.

The inadvertent journey inward.

So I closed my barely open eyes,
and acknowledged
my compromised promise . . .

and I found my Self.

Speak

Our great sin is knowledge.
Knowledge we weren't ready for.
Tears flowing before words,
and answers preceding their questions.

So now the healing we seek
is hidden only in seeking healing.
Our stolen knowledge
only needs context.

So seek.
Seek and heal.

The hopeless endeavor
is somehow the same as the hopeful action.
Only useless words
can spark our great catharsis.

So speak.
Speak and feel.

Come and see
how the river listens.

Drunk at a Concert

Purple light colors the floor.
The concrete sparkles and shines through
the barely lit venue.

While the band plays their songs,
there's no more excuses or distractions.

All that separates us from God
is our shoes.

Playfulness

The zealots pray
with their eyes shut

while the saint's eyes
remain playfully open.

When the children inevitably catch him,
he winks
knowingly.

Normal Miracles

I'm not a big fan of recycled
Christmas music,
but if you are, that's wonderful.
I get it.

When the snow descends for the first time,
there's nothing quite like it.
Everything mundane and routine
is renewed by tiny flakes accumulating.

And like children, we find ourselves
glued to the windows,
awestruck by normal miracles.

Still Healing

book nine

One Paragraph

It was snowing,
so she retired
to the armchair
with blanket and book.

She read one paragraph
and passed out.

What a boring miracle.

Pillow Talk

Two frozen lovers
melt and soak their pillows.
Waking then dreaming,
and waking again.

Hurting and healing,
softened and whittled.
One day, all that remains
will be impossibly simple.

He's an open book
filled with colorful scribbles.
She can ask him anything,
and she's not afraid to.

And when there's nothing to say,
there's something to do.
What color crayon will they choose today?
What is love if it does not play?

The Gift

The Gift is always being given.
So tear it open.

Throw all the meticulously
taped and measured
wrapping paper
all over the floor.

Jump up and down!
Make a snow angel!
Do something that terrifies you
or snuggle up in a blanket instead.

Hold each other close
or let each other go
if need be.

But whatever you do,
just promise me
you won't let this moment
go unnoticed.

So dance to old music
but don't fear a few new songs.
Tell us old stories
but allow us to create new ones.

Because
it's in every breath,
every success,
every failure,
every scar,
every tear,
every family,
every enemy,
and every friend.

The beginning and the end
are both illusions.
This is it. This is the Gift.

True Wisdom

What separates
true wisdom
from empty truisms?

A shit eating grin.

Still Healing

I'm still healing,
but I'm so grateful for this scar.

Oh, what a blessing;
the beauty and futility of this persistent heart.

The Game We Play

Is consistency important?
Should who you are today
be the same as who you were yesterday?

Probably.
But I know you know
that's mostly impossible.

Our identity is our separation
and yet we've convinced ourselves
that it's our salvation.

It's a game we play so often,
that we often forget
it's merely a game.

And it's really not a serious one.

Mostly Rhetorical

The poet speaks
with total abandon
to the ironic futility
of his profession:

Words will always fail,
but it's mostly rhetorical anyway.

We move in circles,
terribly beautiful circles.

Hibernating Poets

The poet awakes
when your young idealist dies,
forgets their name, loses their purpose,
and slowly, inexplicably returns as the weathered,
hopeful pessimist.

There is no one to praise,
and no great name to credit for this transformation.
It just happens. And it's always happening.

Resurrection is quite a quiet, continual affair,
and poets are hibernating everywhere.

Our Perfect Defeat

In the darkness,
you felt something urgent.
One sentence lingered on your lips,
like a residual kiss:

Nothing is ever motionless.

So you left your bed behind
to find no one asleep, all searching
for what they already possess.

Guarded by moonlight,
somewhat safe, somewhat free,
they tried to speak
and lost their voice.

Then they resorted to writing
and lost their pens.
Then they began to sing
and you joined in.

One by one, we botched our melodies
and returned to bed
in an exasperated, perfect defeat.

January

With nostalgic pride,
we look in the wrong direction
and try to spin last year's suffering
as 'divine discipline,'
or some kind of 'cosmic lesson.'

At some point, the past
deserves no more attention.

It's just January.
It's just another month.

So shake the dust
and keep moving.

Resolutions

Another year.
Another winter.
Another mask.

And yet,
She still laughs.

We're all masquerading, dear.
Resolutions do not conquer fears.

The After-Party

No one knew the hour.
But no one dared to check.

The festivities had ended,
but the weight of the witness
suspended us.

Floating on the couch,
we conversed silently,
excitedly. Rigid,
and flowing
among the mess.

Slowly, we float
back down
and know we should begin cleaning.

But instead,
we just watch the snow accumulate outside
until morning's red light.

Back Pain

All that is certain is uncertain,

except for the inevitability of back pain,

and this absurd, lifelong endeavor of healing.

The Implications of Silhouettes

New horizons lie ahead
regardless
of what you leave behind.

Every season ends
with a deep breath
and another courageous dive.

Remember this
and you'll *probably* be alright:

Silhouettes always imply light.

Ephemeral

For us to dance perennial,
some flowers choose to be ephemeral.

Catharsis would never grow
if despair did not flirt with hope.

Perspective's Paradox

The only solution
to the problem of perspective
is empathy.

And yet,

empathy only begins
when both parties accept (begrudgingly),
that all they hold most dearly
is perspective.

No Trumpet

Happiness is quiet.
She requires no ballad,

no trumpet.

She gives herself away
because she knows nothing of herself.
Her cup overflows
because she owns no cup.
Her joy is shared
because it doesn't need to be.

All I will ever see
is right in front of me.
And all that is true
will inevitably
be forgotten...

Only to be remembered again!

So breathe deeply, dear friend.

Our eyes are barely open.

Proof of Wounds

Venerating the doubtful apostle,
countless prayers
pleading for proof of wounds
seem to remain unanswered,

while the tired, blind faithful
grow ever more prideful,
oblique, secluded, and *wounded.*

Blessed are those
who can no longer hide their pain,
for they cannot see their own strength.

And blessed are those
who still believe without sight,
for they cannot see their own bruises.

The Persistence of Principle

In most circumstances,
the persistence of principle alone
should never guarantee

its continuation.

When carefully woven threads
unravel again,
we often forget
there is much more to breathing

than breathing in.

Dance in the Kitchen

The timeless wisdom of the mystics
and the pious chant of the saints
is barely hidden in the morning mist,
and waiting within the softened clay.

This mystery is experienced
when it cannot be explained.

So what are you waiting for?
Make your own fate!

Go to the beach in the dead of winter,
and dance in the kitchen while making dinner.

Take what you're given, and give in return.
Breathe when you can, and seek when you hurt.

Learn a new language,
but start with the swear words.
Call up old lovers, and go on blind dates.

Open dusty drawers full of old treasures,
hold them close and then throw them away.

Face fears together,
take on new adventures,
own up to your failures,
and give yourself a new name
if you must!

Let it be enough.

Let it be enough.

Let it be enough.

Steam

She is rising
through acrylic rings,
steeped and warm,
wispy and flowing.

Bravely calm,
she caresses my palm
as my thumb rhythmically
circles her mug.

I am reading under lamplight
and immediately losing
every word.
How absurd!

The Red Rug

It's full of patterns,
shapes and textures.

If you're not careful
you'll trip,
(like you always do),
and its many swirls
and sinews
will swallow you whole.

Like us,
it's full of diamonds
and rough edges,
but it's soft to the touch.

Soon enough,
your eyes will adjust
and follow the table
to escape its hypnotic angles
and return to the real world.

But upon returning,
you'll be smirking;
you were subconsciously curling your toes.

Snowball Fights in May

Some snow doesn't melt until June.
And somehow, new flowers still bloom.

So I'm done wasting these days away
wishing for different days.

I cannot wait
for snowball fights in May...

But I'm definitely not ready
to accept
the tragic irony of this one.

Still Dreaming

book ten

Sowing

Every spring,
new seeds are planted
in old, open space;

the prelude to praise.

Waking Rituals

Wake up.
Check your email
without responding.

I'm half asleep.
I'm still dreaming.

Wake up.
Wash your hair
but not your feet.

I'm still not ready
to leave.

Wake up.
Clean your frames
with this alcohol wipe.

Wake up
without caffeine.
There's never enough time
for coffee.

I'm still dreaming.
I'm still running late.

And it's only Monday.

Watching the Flowers Bloom

You're gazing at the stars,
a billion blazing fires,
still searching for old sparks.

You're singing with the moon,
a beautiful melody,
still waiting for the Spirit to fill the room.

You're speaking in tongues,
dancing beyond language,
and still searching for translations.

My love, you're thinking too much.
I AM watching the flowers bloom.

Stillness

All that grows is all that moves.

But sometimes, stillness is a necessary ruse.

True Solitude

He who is already convinced
that he stands alone
won't recognize his own shadow.

True solitude is communal.

What You Were Looking For

After the dust settles
and his war is lost again,
the seeker returns
to the harshly kind words
of his impossibly patient lover.

Although he is still far from arriving,
she runs out to meet him in the dirt;
surrendering the integrity of her white skirt.

And before the dust settles,
she playfully (and somewhat condescendingly)
implores him with a squeeze and a kiss:

"Did you find what you were looking for?"

"Of course not!"

he replies with a wink and a half-smile,
once again losing himself in her wary eyes.

Birdsong

The wisdom of the birdsong
is neither her melody nor her solace.

It's her persistence.

Her irreverent laments
in the dark night of her heart,
carry on until the morning

where they inexplicably
become reverent again
without missing a single beat.

Rest

Every few thousand breaths or so,
it would be beneficial to recall the miracle
of the habitual movement of our chest
by simply holding our breath
for a minute or so.

Real rest is often
an uncomfortable repose.

Golden Joineries

Yet again,
we try and fail to comprehend
each other's actions
and suffer the consequences;
shattering into tearful pieces.

But mutual exasperation
is a necessary frustration
in the art of reconnection.

True compassion
is not amalgamation.

At the deep ledges of self,
empathy bridges the abyss
and mends our brokenness
by tearfully highlighting it.

Revolutions

Most of today's
sacred songs
were once played
with playful irreverence,

and the grimaces
of the traditional
were overcome
by the smirks of the young.

Every revolution is fated
to merely flirt with freedom.

So, together we rotate
in terribly beautiful circles,
hopefully gravitating
towards some kind of center.

Synesthesia

I cannot see your colors.
I don't have synesthesia.

But your music moves me
all the same.

Overlapping Parts

Promising each other
impossible things,
with fingers crossing
and stitching together,

two warm figures
inch ever closer
under the blue light
of the street lamp,

overflowing with the fantasy
of convictions and ambitions,
rapidly beating hearts,
and so many overlapping parts.

In a few hours, however,
the same two figures will wake
to exchange routine greetings
under the amber light of morning,

overwhelmed with the reality
of obligations and agreements,
steady beating hearts,
and so many overlapping parts.

Resurrections

The resurrections we seek
are not miraculous interventions,
but continuous decisions

with grace bridging its seasons.

The dead man doesn't need to breathe;
he chooses to breathe.
Some days, he stays dead.

But that's quite alright.

Vacancy

One light
is casting two shadows
extending from your feet
forming some kind of ‘V’
like an arrow
collapsing inward.

Maybe
the darkness of their vacancy
is revealing their fullness;

like a verse preceding a chorus.

The Cosmic Joke

The painter ponders
infinite brushstrokes,
accidentally discovers
the cosmic joke,
laughs a hearty laugh
and goes home,
with bleary red eyes
and a curious smirk.

But he leaves a light on
as he goes.

And now his empty canvas
glows
like a summer snowstorm.

Momentary Melting

Singing along to a new song
with an oddly familiar timbre,
we melted together
and remembered the freedom of dancing.

Approximately three minutes later, however,
like ice from water,
we froze back into our bodies again
and remembered the miracle of stillness.

Within every performance
of a true melody,
revelations long forgotten
are rediscovered
and then discarded
to be rediscovered again.

In His Image

Stand between two mirrors
facing each other
and then close your eyes.

Do you still believe
you are reflecting infinitely?

Distant Refrains

She placed the needle on the record
and walked away.
But curiously enough,

her distant refrains
rearrange us
anyway.

The Supposed Scarcity of Plenty

It doesn’t take much
to break the surface tension
and drown in the depths within.

An Interpretation of 1 Corinthians 13:11

This spark of being,
this shared condition,
this inherent desperation,
is all that is needed to begin.

But careful curation
and copious cooperation
within endless conflict
is all that is needed to continue.

Glints

The Holy Ghost remains
humbly hidden,
and would be impossible to find
if not for her occasional glints
sparkling through the fading geodes of our eyes.

Like Roads Always Do

The road forks ahead
like roads always do.

So hold me close
for one more day,

and tomorrow morning,
we must part ways.

I know.
I'm terrified too.

But we must uncover the courage
to see this through.

The Friend with an Outstretched Hand

For our own good, we can only squint
at the overwhelming light of incarnation.
And I can only attempt to further explain this
with this simple illustration.

Because in the impossibly endless moment
that you decide to accept his offer,
the solace you've been seeking your entire life
rushes over you like a river
and you're content to drown in its current.

But just as suddenly as it came,
this infinite river vanishes
when skin touches skin;
though it still re-frames.

Persistence

Regardless, we persist
as we've always been:

broken, healed,
and admirably foolish.

Eroding Convictions

He drew a line in the sand,
but then the tide came in
and washed it away.

So he shed a tear and shrugged,
and went swimming
with those he used to blame
for his suffering.

After the erosion,
there are no more enemies.

LP

I know you know this,
but I'll say it anyway.
Endings are boring.
Endings are unrealistic.
They never actually happen.

Our story is never fully told
because our story never fully ends.
Our truest selves
are all but hints and clues;
dirty windows to look through.

Like an old record,
we are Long Playing.
A call and response.
A groove and a needle.

And we still spin at the center.

A Benediction of Fertilization

She bought a letter board,
but it only came with six letters:
3 vowels and 3 consonants.
After much deliberation,
she discerned the board could only read,

"BE SOIL."

Years later,
after finally uncovering all that's hidden within,
she arrives at her final pages.
Surrounded by family and friends,
she submits to the warm regret of her own blindness,
accepts her hopelessly hopeful human condition,
and finally becomes soil.

But right before she goes,
she gifts us with this benediction:

"We can only make meaning out of what we're given,
and there remains so much left to learn.
But take heart! What dies has a tendency to fertilize
endless new chapters."

Still Squinting

doxologies

It's All Music

It's all right here.

It's only hidden because
our eyes are barely open.

We can't hear it yet,
but it's all music.
It's all learning to listen.

The Love Story

Her husband grew blind
so she closed her eyes.

All we lose
is all we find.

An Epigraph

I know, I know.
Epigraphs usually go at the beginnings of things.
But this is exactly the point I've been trying to make:
Every ending is also a beginning.

I know that sounds terribly cliche, (it is)
and perhaps you're tired of me
repeating myself at this point,
but just bear with me for one last nail in the coffin.

It's all beyond language,
and it's even beyond symbols.
But sometimes symbols and language
help us understand it a little better.
One such symbol that has aided
my own understanding is an old Celtic one
called a "triskelion."

This symbol is quite simple.
It's just three interconnected spirals.
You can see it below:

It means "movement."
But not just any kind of movement.
It's a movement towards a better understanding.
But it's also learning that this kind of movement
means accepting that you'll never arrive anywhere
other than
right where you've always been.

It's moving in circles.
It's moving from life to death and to resurrection,
and from resurrection to life and to death again.

It's opening our eyes in the morning
and closing them in the evening.
But it's also learning that on average,
our eyes are never fully open.

And with each new day,
we're still learning,
still drowning,
still dancing,
still yearning,
still healing
still dreaming,

and still squinting.

"At the first level of the path
he saw mountains as mountains
and rivers as rivers.

On the second level of the path
he saw that mountains are not mountains
and rivers are not rivers.

And at a third level
he saw once again mountains were mountains
and rivers were rivers."

- Qingyuan Weixin

© 2021 Andrew Wesselhoff

www.ingramcontent.com/pod-product-compliance
Lightning Source LLC
LaVergne TN
LVHW091211150826
845672LV00005B/1312
* 9 7 9 8 7 4 1 0 8 2 3 1 7 *